AF338139

MAMMALS GUIDE BOOK

FROM A TO F

Mammals for Kids Encyclopedia
Children's Mammal Books

Speedy Publishing LLC

40 E. Main St. #1156

Newark, DE 19711

www.speedypublishing.com

Copyright 2017

All Rights reserved. No part of this book may be reproduced or used in any way or form or by any means whether electronic or mechanical, this means that you cannot record or photocopy any material ideas or tips that are provided in this book.

Welcome to the world of mammals! Mammals can be tiny or large, live on land or in the sea, and sometimes look pretty strange. Let's visit a selection of mammals whose names begin with the letters A to F.

WHAT MAKES A MAMMAL?

Mammals are one class of animals on the planet Earth. They have some things in common:

- 🐾 They have glands that create milk that the parent can provide to feed its young when the babies are small.
- 🐾 They have fur or hair. Even whales and dolphins, mammals that have adapted to life at sea, have tufts of fine hair near their mouths.

- They are warm-blooded.
- Almost all mammals have teeth. Anteaters are the exception!

There are over five thousand species of mammals, and they live in almost every climate on Earth. Some, like humans, can adapt so they can live everywhere, while some other mammals may only be found on one island, or in a particular type of forest.

The largest mammal is the blue whale, the largest animal that has ever lived on Earth. It roams all the oceans of the world.

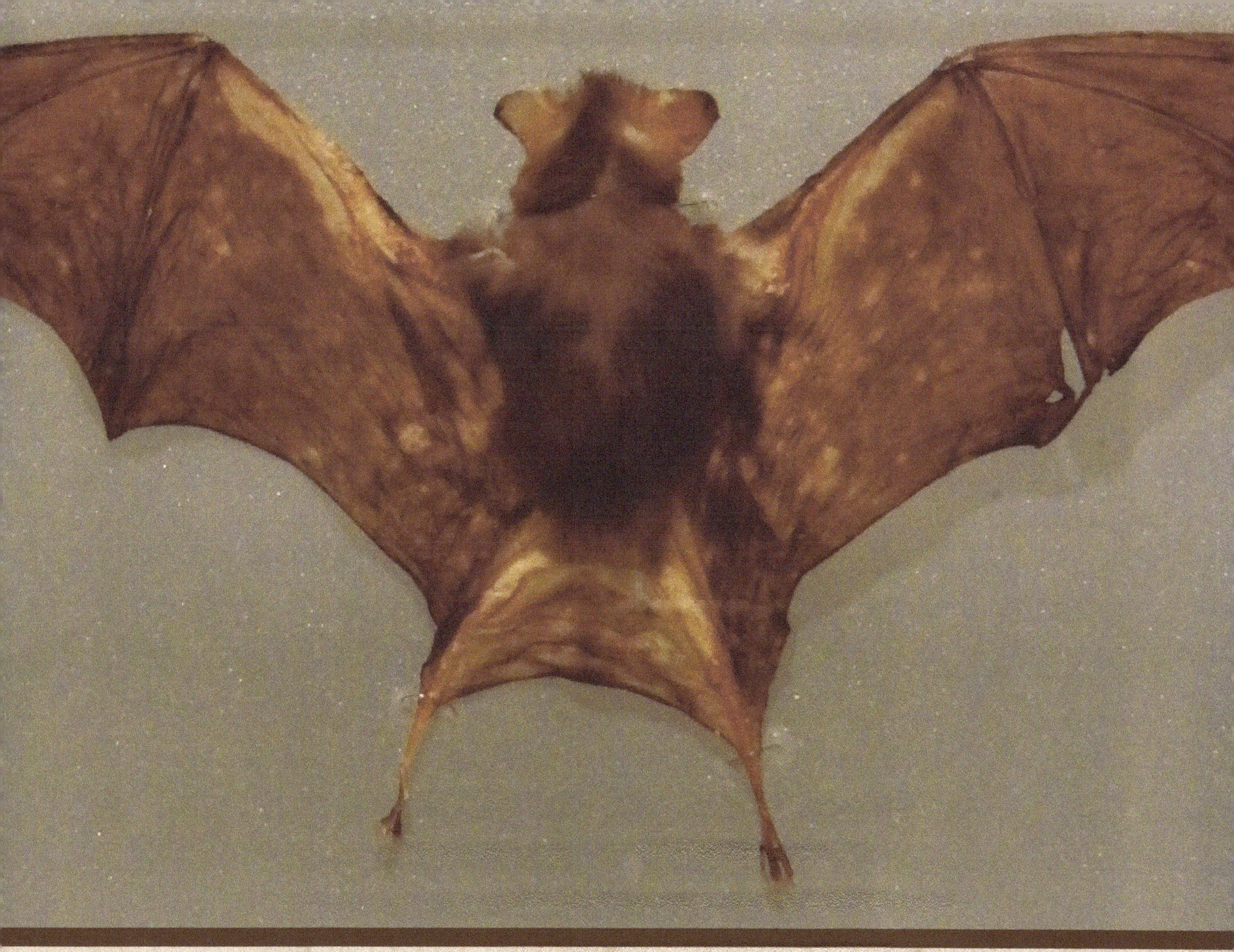

The smallest mammal we know of is the Kitti's hog-nosed bat, also known as the bumblebee bat because it is so tiny. It only lives in certain forests in Thailand.

Humans are mammals. So every creature you see in this book is a distant relative of yours!
MAKE YOUR NIGHTS

SÓ ÔNIBUS
6 - 22h
Mantenha
Sua Cidade Limpa

AARDVARK

AARDVARK

The aardvark lives in Africa and is rarely seen because it sleeps through the day and only comes out to feed at night. It has sharp claws for digging holes in the sides of termite and ant nests, and then it uses its long, sticky tongue to scoop up hundreds or thousands of insects in a single meal. Aardvarks can be as large as a large dog, but they are very shy and are not dangerous to people.

AFRICAN WILD DOG

This dog species is also known as the "painted wolf". African wild dogs hunt in packs and were once common in South Africa; but with the growth of cities and towns, and the decline of the animals they like to hunt, they are becoming endangered. They are very intelligent and coordinate well when a pack hunts an animal.

AFRICAN WILD DOG

ALPACA

Alpacas live in the Andes Mountains of South America. They are part of the camel family, and their closest relatives are guanacos, llamas, and vicuñas. People make lovely warm clothing from alpaca fur.

AYE-AYE

This lemur species lives only on the island of Madagascar. It hunts insects at night, using its long middle finger to dig its food out of the bark of trees and spaces between rocks.

Because local people believe the Aye-Aye brings bad luck, it has been hunted almost out of existence.

BLACK RHINOCEROS

BLACK RHINOCEROS

Black rhinos mainly eat plants, but are short-sighted and unpredictable and can attack people, other animals, and even cars and trains without much warning. The few remaining black rhinos live in isolated areas in east and south Africa.

BLUE WHALE

The blue whale is larger than any dinosaur that ever lived, making it the size champion of Earth. Blue whales were moving toward extinction fifty years ago, but a ban on hunting them for food and for whale oil means that the species is slowly growing to sustainable numbers again. Learn more about them in the Baby Professor book Have You Ever Seen a Blue Whale?

BONGO

The bongo is a beautiful, shy antelope that lives in forests in central Africa. As its habitat shrinks, and because it is hunted as a trophy animal and for food, bongos are now extremely rare.

BONOBO

The bonobo, or "pygmy chimpanzee" is a great ape that lives in one rain forest in central Africa. Although it looks a bit like a chimpanzee, bonobos have a different social system and lifestyle than chimps do.

One significant difference is that bonobos seem to work out their differences through acts of affection, rather than fighting with each other.

The brown bear, or "grizzly bear", can be found in forests across the northern United States and in Canada. On the Pacific coast, they can be found fishing for salmon as the fish leap up rapids and waterfalls on their way upstream to spawn.

BABIRUSA

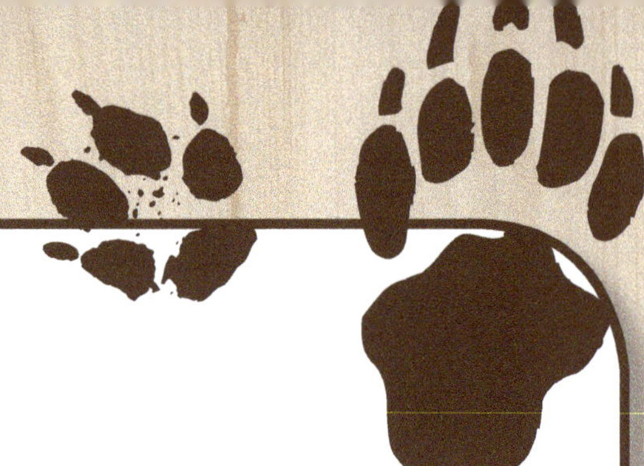

The babirusa is a wild pig that lives in tropical forests on the island of Sulawesi, east of Borneo, and on other islands nearby. It has been hunted for food and for its tusks so much that it is now very rare. The male's upper tusks curve up through holes in its snout, back toward its head.

BABIRUSA

BROWN HYENA

Brown hyenas are active at night in southern Africa, and are very stealthy so humans rarely see them. They live in packs led by the senior female, and are excellent scavengers.

They often eat from the carcasses of animals that other hunters have killed and left partly-eaten. They have strong jaws and teeth for crunching up bones so they can eat the marrow.

LEAF NOSED BAT

BATS

There are over one thousand bat species, which is over 20 percent of all the mammal species on Earth, so it is hard to single one out as the most interesting. The rarest, as mentioned, is the bumblebee bat. Perhaps the most dramatic-looking is Townsend's Big-eared Bat. They roost upside down in caves by day, coming out in the evening to hunt flying insects and even small mammals. They emit high-pitched sounds and navigate by the echo of the sound coming back to them.

CHEETAH

The cheetah is the fastest mammal in the world over short distances. It can chase down speedy animals like antelopes. Cheetahs used to be seen throughout Africa and western Asia, but its range and population are much smaller now. Cheetahs often hunt in pairs, with two brothers attacking the same prey from different angles.

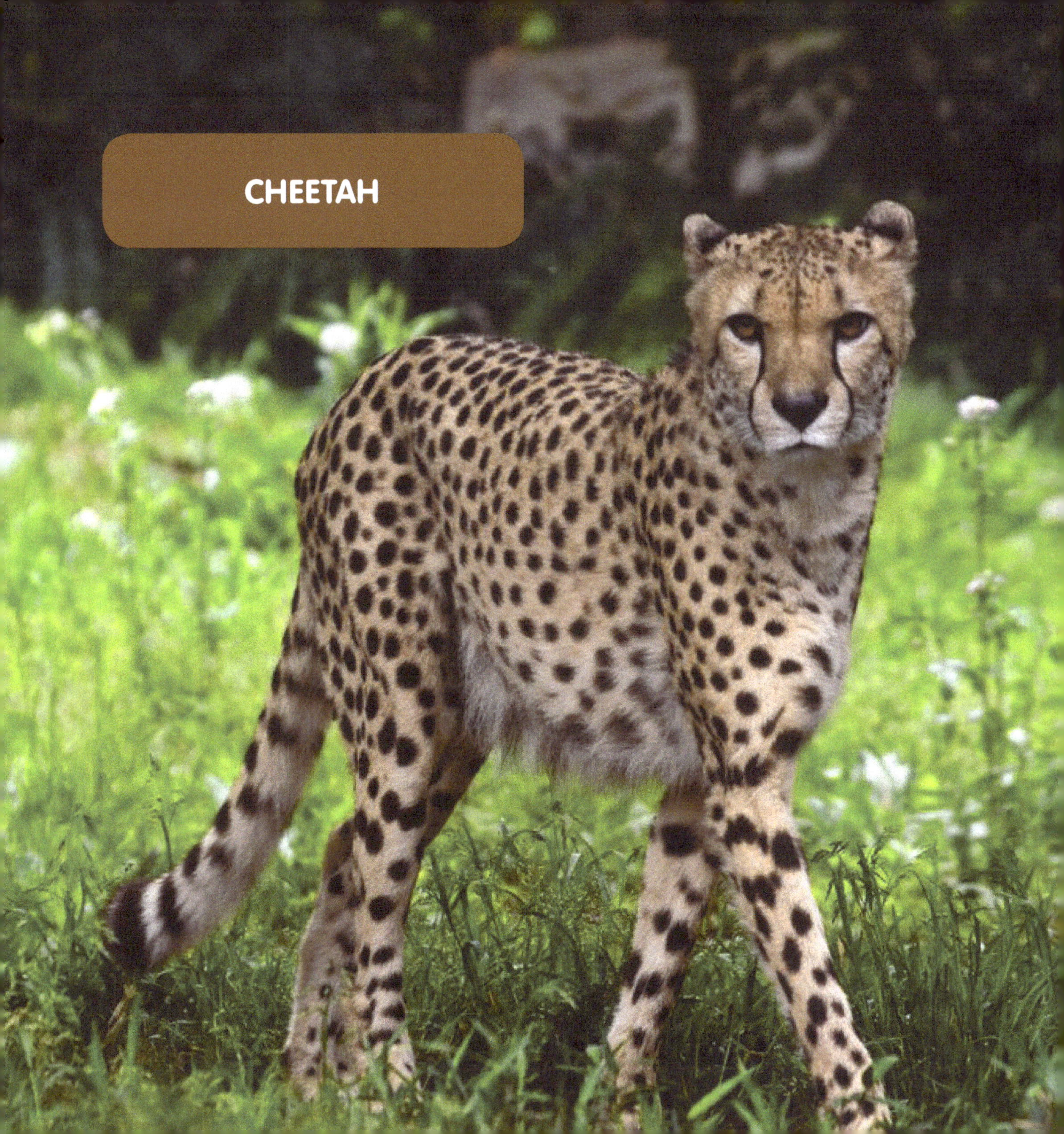
CHEETAH

CHIMPANZEE

Chimps are our closest relatives, and lots of people see them in zoos around the world. However, they are harder to find in their natural home, the lowland forests of central Africa.

ou are more likely to hear them than to see one! Chimps make a sleeping nest each night, and then move to a new location each day. They have a complex social system and are highly territorial.

A LAZY CLOUDED LEOPARD

CLOUDED LEOPARD

There are two species of this lovely feline, halfway between the great and small cats. They have beautiful fur but stay hidden from humans in the forests of mainland Asia and the islands of Borneo and Sumatra. They spend much of their lives high in trees, and tend to be active at night.

COLUGO

Colugos are sometimes called "flying lemurs", although they aren't lemurs and don't fly! They are gliding mammals, like very large flying squirrels, but with a head that is shaped sort of like the head of a deer (but with no horns).

Colugos live in the forests of Borneo and some Philippine islands, and tend to hunt at sunset and into the evening, like bats.

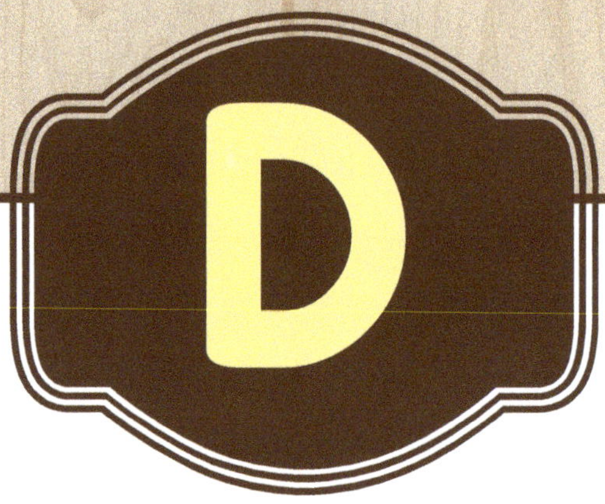

DIK-DIK

There are four species of dik-diks in eastern and southern Africa. They are small antelopes, very graceful and fast. They get their name from the alarm cry the females make when they sense danger. Both males and females also make a high-pitched whistling noise to warn of predators.

DIK-DIK

DOLPHIN

There are more than forty species of dolphins, most of them living in the warmer parts of the world's oceans. Some rare dolphin species prefer fresh water in rivers. Dolphins are highly intelligent, fast-moving, and seem to express both playfulness and affection.

DUGONG

Dugongs are enormous ocean mammals that live on vegetable matter in the coastal waters from the east coast of Africa to Australia. They can be as long as a grown human is tall, but can weigh as much as one thousand pounds.

Early sightings of them by seafarers may have been the source of stories about "mermaids" in the ocean. Their nearest relative on land is the elephant.

ECHIDNA

ECHIDNA

There are four types of echidnas, also known as "spiny anteaters", in Australia, parts of New Guinea, and on some other islands in the area. They, along with the duck-billed platypus, are the only mammals who lay eggs rather than giving live birth to their young!

ELEPHANT

Elephants are the largest land animals since the time of the wooly mammoths in the last ice age. There are three main species, two in Africa and one in Asia, but all three populations are under threat from poachers and destruction of their habitat.

ADORABLE FERRET

FERRET

Ferrets are relatives of weasels. In England, they are often kept as hunting animals and used to hunt rabbits in the fields or rats around the farm.

FOSSA

 **T**he fossa is the largest predator on the island of Madagascar. It hunts other animals both by day and by night, but as the forest shrinks because of human activity, its numbers are declining.

POACHING

CREATURES IN DANGER

Although we share this world with all the other mammals, humans have not been very good at making sure all mammals continue to be welcome on the Earth.

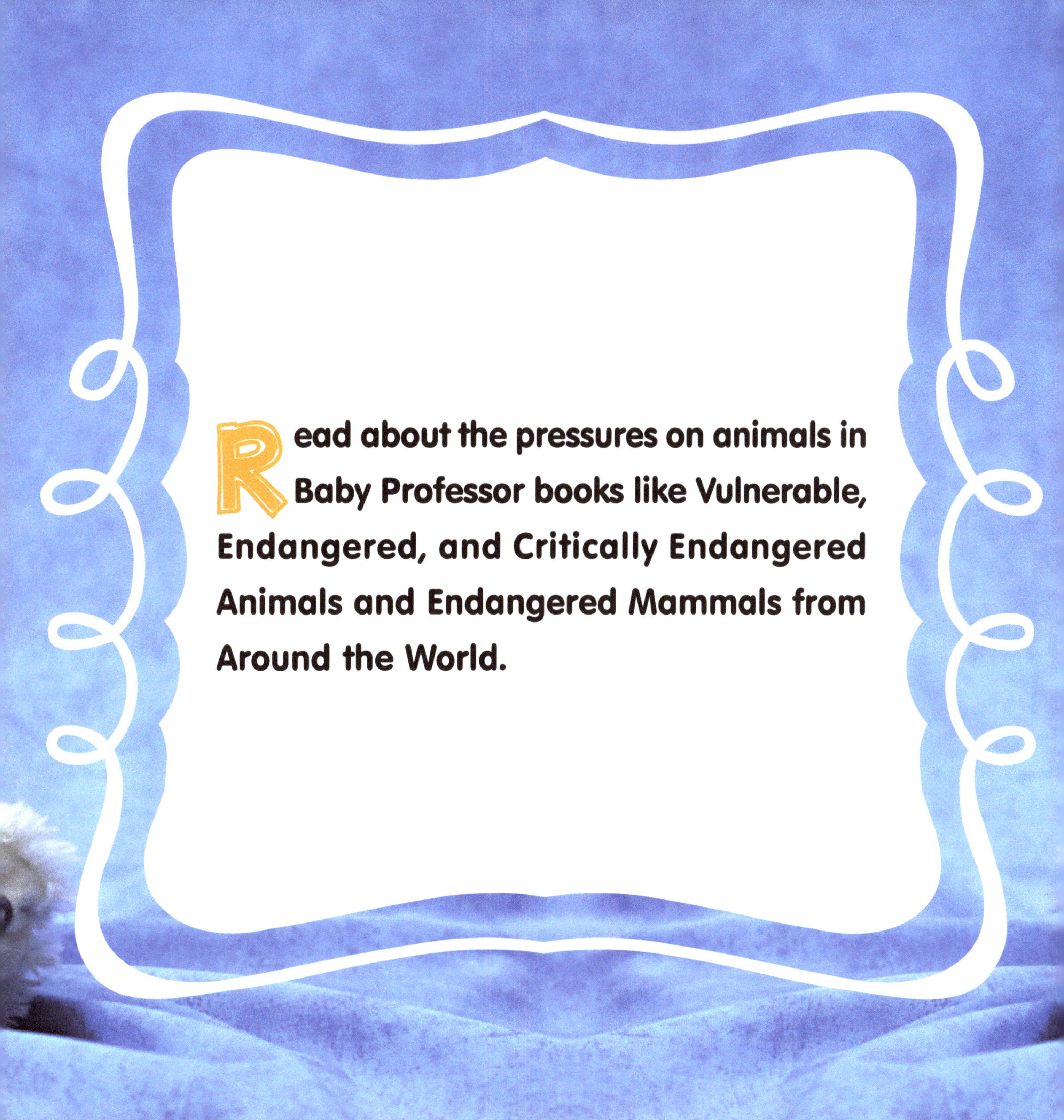

Read about the pressures on animals in Baby Professor books like Vulnerable, Endangered, and Critically Endangered Animals and Endangered Mammals from Around the World.

Visit
BABY PROFESSOR
EDUCATION KIDS
www.BabyProfessorBooks.com
to download Free Baby Professor eBooks
and view our catalog of new and exciting
Children's Books

www.ingramcontent.com/pod-product-compliance
Lightning Source LLC
Chambersburg PA
CBHW041936110726
48010CB00003B/122